D1563008

CULTIVATING CULTURE

AS A GARDEN

REAPING THE HARVEST OF DIVERSITY & INCLUSION

By DR. NICOLE D. PRICE *with* JOEL BARRETT

LIVELY
PARADOX

Cover & Book Design: Ashley Gaffney Design
Editing: Linda Odell
Cultivating Culture as a Garden by Nicole D. Price with Joel Barrett – 1st ed.

CULTIVATING CULTURE

AS A GARDEN

REAPING THE HARVEST OF DIVERSITY & INCLUSION

By DR. NICOLE D. PRICE *with* JOEL BARRETT

LIVELY
PARADOX

TABLE OF CONTENTS

PART ONE: The Garden

PART TWO: Which Role Do You Play?

PART THREE: Assessments

THE HARVEST IS PLENTIFUL BUT THE LABORERS ARE FEW.

— Matthew 9:35

INTRODUCTION

Our established practice has been to tout the benefits of diversity, equity, and inclusion without truly discussing the work that is necessary to reap that harvest. Diversity, equity, and inclusion drives good outcomes, but we cannot randomly throw difference into a culture and expect that we will be rewarded with greater innovation, decreased costs, improved service and better quality. We must cultivate our culture in order for a garden of diversity, equity, and inclusion to flourish. The garden is a metaphor that can help us understand the requirements and roles necessary to develop a culture of diversity, equity and inclusion in an organization. In the garden, various species of plants – lettuce, tomatoes, peppers and the like –grow side by side successfully, each enhancing the whole when it's time to harvest ingredients for a fresh summer salad. With flowers to decorate the table, too! But as anyone who gardens knows, that harvest does not magically appear. It requires planning, nurturing and sustained maintenance to yield the desired results. So, too, the successful effort to bring to our organizations a flourishing culture of diversity, equity, and inclusion.

W hy is cultivating such an important factor in gardening? How and when should we cultivate? Cultivating is a time-honored gardening principle and, like many things that are long standing, is easy to understand. The practice of cultivating the soil basically serves two purposes: loosening the soil to optimize the retention and penetration of air, water, and nutrients; and removing weeds. Cultivating breaks up the crusty soil of indifference, exclusion and injustice that naturally rests under the surface in all of us. If we don't actively work on creating a culture of diversity, equity, and inclusion, we won't have access to nutrients necessary for inclusivity to survive.

Before you take on a culture-building garden, you need to look into your heart, clarify your goals, and ask yourself some questions.

1. Define what you actually want to grow in your garden.

2. Why do you want to grow and cultivate anything?

3. Confirm that you truly want what you say you intend to grow.

— Do you just want tomatoes for summer family dinners?

— Do you want to can them for chili and salsa through the winter?

— Are you intending to sell to a produce distributor?

Because being conscious of what you want and why is essential to creating the right conditions. The "right" conditions for some objectives may well be completely wrong for others. If you're just planting a garden because somebody told you to (such as checking off a performance review box), or you want to look cool now that "local food" is a thing, or if you honestly don't even like tomatoes and don't care if they grow or not, it's a waste of time. Be aware, of course if you don't commit to this work, you'll eventually end up hungry.

But if you've answered the questions and have committed to proceeding, you're ready to tackle the three primary elements required to reap the benefits of diversity, equity, and inclusion. In the context of culture as a garden, there are three primary components to consider: tilling the soil, planting the seeds, and tending to the weeds. You must also determine whether your location provides the right environment for success.

CHOOSING THE LOCATION

I am a terrible gardener. I have never been able to actually grow anything outside in the soil. However, my grandmother could grow everything. She grew vegetables and herbs, fruit on trees and vines, and she loved to tend to her garden. I remember the year she encouraged me to grow bell peppers. It was one of the hottest summers on record in Missouri. I bought the plants, chose great soil, and was eager with excitement. Those bell peppers were no match for two things – my inattention and the Midwest heat. My little peppers died a swift and pitiful death. The lesson I learned: Regardless of where you decide to plant your garden, the conditions must be able to support it.

My pepper "garden" represents our organizations. Real organizations. Organizations primarily in the Midwest but they can legitimately be anywhere. I have been a consultant for more than a decade and have had the opportunity to watch well-meaning people tout that they are going to tackle diversity, equity, and inclusion initiatives. Many times, the people engaging me work in a diversity division or department (sometimes a department of one). They are hopeful. They are eager. After all, they have at least been given a budget and an edict! They think they can get people to get along, despite their differences, once and for all.

My first questions? How is the soil? What's the sun like? Do you have a water source? Fertile environments have three characteristics.

THE CORRECT TEMPERATURE: What is the external climate like? Is the temperature good for seed planting? Seeds tend to stay dormant until the temperature is right. Consequently, we have to focus on our culture and identify what needs to be done in to create the climate for diversity, equity, and inclusion to thrive.

GOOD LOCATION: Not every organization, small or large, is the place for every type of diversity to thrive. Deciding to plant seeds must be balanced with where to plant them. Planting seeds in the wrong location may hinders success now, and jeopardize future efforts as well.

WATER: All "seeds" (and people) have a thirst to grow and germinate, and there must be a both social desire and a source of water -- budget, people, long-term commitment -- to quench that thirst.

There are some places where the conditions just aren't right. So, before you begin, be sure you have decent conditions for throwing a bunch of people together to work through challenges. Decent conditions include having:

1. At least 10% of your leadership is interested in pursuing diversity and inclusion efforts. They understand the value and are invested in making it happen.

2. No more than 10% of your organization is completely opposed to diversity and inclusion efforts. There will be naysayers, but they must not represent a critical mass to actively or passively resist your efforts.

3. Resources to support people when they get stuck.

4. Some idea of what good looks like (Some people refer to this as a plan).

Choose your location wisely. You don't want your work or your organization to suffer the same fate as my failed pepper garden.

FIRST, TILLING THE SOIL

The purpose of tilling is to mix organic matter into your soil, help control weeds and break up hardened soil, or loosen up a small area for planting. A farmer or gardener does not till or break up the soil too deeply. In fact, with regard to depth, less is better. When introducing diversity of any kind to an environment, think of the newness as embarking upon new soil. If you are going to plant in an area that has not been cultivated before, the ground must be tilled.

There are some situations where diversity is welcomed and celebrated. There are other instances in which the environment is not quite ready. If the latter is the case, the person who represents diversity (no matter the difference) must adjust his or her style in order to be seen and heard.

Soil tillers are the pioneers. Although it is hard work (and wholly unfair), sometimes pioneers have to assimilate in order to be a catalyst for advancement. They must actively adjust to make space and room to cultivate the new, different, and better.

Cultivating the soil is backbreaking work that only a small number of people have the tolerance to endure. But their work makes it easier for newly germinated seeds to sprout through the surface of the soil. Similarly, breaking up the existing culture allows different employees to blossom in the future. Consider what would happen if the soil hasn't been tilled and a person of difference jumps in with weed-killer at this point in the process. Long-term damage would be inevitable.

I have seen this happen time and time again. To progress the organization's diversity and inclusion efforts, recruiters seek someone who "gets it" so they hire the most radical and revolutionary person they can find to turn the place around. But too often, they have not been honest with the new recruit. Consequently, the new recruit comes to the organization with grandiose plans, only to run into the brick wall of resistance. They share their plans thinking everyone is on board, when in reality the only person who knows about their business transformation plans is their direct boss and NO. ONE. ELSE. In fact, the hiring manager likely thinks she or he can just throw the new recruit into the fray and achieve the desired results.

The ensuing cycle is consistent. The new recruit does exactly what was asked. The team pushes back complaining to HR at every turn. The HR department sends someone to "coach" the new recruit, who may or may not understand what is happening but usually continues to present diversity and inclusion best practices. The manager and the HR department decide that the new recruit is not a "cultural fit" then terminate that employee claiming that the work was unsuccessful. In other words, the individual brought in to be a change-maker – a tiller – is deemed to be a bad fit – a weed.

Because weed killers have a specific purpose – killing vegetation – involving them at the tilling phase runs the risk of creating an environment where nothing can grow. Soil tillers are important. They prep the climate for diverse perspectives to thrive later (emphasis on later). I'll admit,

I don't like it. I want to cut straight to yanking out toxic weeds. But that's because I'm not a tiller. I don't have the temperament to be a tiller.

However, you recognize tillers when you hear their names. Dr. Dorothy Height was a tiller. She was the only woman allowed on the stage (other than Mahalia Jackson, who was there to sing) during Rev. Dr. Martin Luther King's "I Have a Dream" speech. It is important to note that Dr. Dorothy Height, in all her brilliance and strength, was not permitted to speak.

Now imagine if you would trying to put Alexandria Ocasio Cortez, or "AOC" as she's called, on that stage. Yeah. She's not going if she can't speak. Women like Dr. Height were the tillers who prepared the soil for the likes of AOC. So let's hear it for the tillers, who deserve our respect for the bumps and bruises they sustain as they establish an environment for the work to come.

SECOND, PLANTING SEEDS

S eeds, like people, naturally grow and thrive in fertile environments. Here's the thing, though: that soil has been worked over by the tillers, who have most likely added manure and other fertilizer to improve its conditions. Speaking plainly, someone put up with a lot of sh*t before the planters arrived.

Planting is still hard work, but it's work built on the previous efforts of others. As they go about their tasks, planters may forget all the work that has been done to make planting seeds possible.

According to Gallup, leaders are responsible for up to 70% of the climate of engagement in their organizations. In other words, leaders are the ones who help to establish situations in which all three conditions are met and seeds can flourish. Most leaders are planters. They want to create a great culture, but regularly hope and wish that a culture of diversity, equity, and inclusion will merely happen without their effort. But things just don't work that way, because a workplace culture of diversity, equity, and inclusion must be intentional. Intentionality plants seeds in fertile soil and encourages others to share their perspectives, fosters ambitious ideas, and encourages creativity.

Planting feels good because if it is done correctly, you will see the fruit of your labor. You will see different people succeeding at the highest levels of the organization. You will start to see gender parity. The boards, commissions, and other decision-making bodies will start to reflect the community in which organizations operate.

Sounds great, huh? Not so fast. When they start to see progress in the planting phase, planters themselves start to feel the need to take rest breaks. I am all for wellness breaks. However, when the breaks become retirement villas where we just move in and live off of the harvest the result is predictable. WEEDS. TAKE. OVER. You can't just till and plant or your garden will be taken over by weeds.

While it's not always easy to see, I have also encountered this phenomenon often in my consulting work. Here are some examples:

- 1,500 women show up for an annual conference designed to provide additional leadership opportunities for women. So, the next year, you decide to rename the conference to be gender-neutral -- not so that gender nonconforming people could feel included, but rather so that "men would feel more comfortable" coming.

- Once marriage equality legislation is passed, an LBGT chamber of commerce decides that is evidence enough to remove the social justice component of their mission.

- Legislation expanding access to health care and de-privatizing prisons is passed, giving one million more United States citizens access to basic health care and releasing another one million from prison. Then in the next election cycle more people decide that voting for president is no longer a requirement of good citizenship. You know? Feels like socialism.

- 99.9988% of presidents and vice presidents in all of United States history have been White, yet when one Black person is elected to the office over 200 years after the country's founding, we proclaim ourselves to be in a post-racial America, and use that term enough that you actually know what I'm talking about.

- 35 of the Fortune 500 CEO are women so it is suggested that we are making gender progress. Never mind that, at the current rate of progress, it will take more than 200 years to see 250 of those 500 CEO's to be women.

The changes we seek are not inconsequential. They are incremental. As such, we must build on incremental progress. Each of the aforementioned examples demonstrate a tendency of making a little bit of progress, then quitting your job as a farmer because you have "done the work" and you are "tired." This work requires a continual reset and restart. You can't keep starting over.

Dr. Ibram X. Kendi said it in simple and clear terms – progress is followed by regression. Why? Because weeds don't take breaks. Weeds don't need proper conditions to grow. They don't need much except for space. You can't make space for weeds in your garden. They take over.

FINALLY, WEEDING

There is a patch of rocks in my driveway. No earthly thing should grow there. I've already told you I live in the Midwest. The summers in my city can be excruciating. Temperatures in July and August rise to over 100 degrees Fahrenheit. Now add rocks! The rocks hold heat and have scorched even my potted plants if I don't water them often and early in the morning. Want to know what can grow there? Weeds!

First, we have to understand that weeds exist – and most likely exist in your organization. Inclusion does not mean that all voices are heard and that all perspectives are honored. Inclusion means that all perspectives that are driven by bringing everyone along are heard. By definition, that means that hateful language, and more importantly discriminatory policies and practices, must be weeded out of an organization.

What is the purpose of weeding? Weeds are unwanted because they are unsightly or crowd out the light from the attitudes, behaviors and mindsets we want our associates to experience. They also rob nutrients from the seeds that are planted. In other words, if the weeds of hate are allowed to flourish, we signal to the culture that we do not take our roles as cultivators of culture seriously.

Weeds always inhibit growth within the garden. Accordingly, we need weed pullers and we need them to go deep because hate, unconscious bias and discriminatory practices are not usually hanging around on the surfaces of our organization. These things are usually hidden deep beneath the soil. Weed killers pluck hate and 'isms' and 'ogynies' out of our culture from their roots, recognizing that doing otherwise (or nothing) could allow it them to take over. We must exercise the courage required to address these ills before they destroy the goodness that is inherent in most people. Consequently, confront problems, remove distractions, and resolve any conflicts. And do it without delay.

Weed pullers must be cautious, though. Because while pulling the weeds is essential, we need to check in every now and then, to ensure we are not improperly assigning the "weed" category. Weed pullers have to align with partners who are able to see potential value in what has been defined as a weed, and consider adding it to the garden plan IF it can produce complementary benefits. The ultimate example, of course, is the tiller hired to be a culture change-maker (cited previously) who was misunderstood as a weed and terminated. And dandelions could be seen as weeds unless you're aware of their medicinal use or even their use as garden greens for salads. If you're growing tomatoes for a café and could use dandelion greens in a fabulous new salad, grow and develop them instead of throwing them away. There's a fine line here between letting bad stuff germinate and throwing out good stuff you hadn't originally intended, so this is where your earlier work defining the "what" and "why" of your efforts is important to revisit.

This determination requires human involvement, empathy and compassion. Try not to take the Roundup™ Approach - squirt Roundup™ over everything and kill the whole garden (or the people eating the garden's bounty!) with the weeds. See people with caring eyes and talk with people to ensure that their positions are educated. I know this is hard to believe but I have held some pretty "weedy" opinions when I was ill-informed.

In my consulting experience, weed pullers tend to be consultants rather than employees. We need them operating in various roles. Unfortunately, many organizations can't withstand someone on the internal team who is consistently lifting up the rocks and pointing out the dirty worms. As such, organizations pay for someone to come in every once in a while to give a peek and then send them on their way.

It is also important to know that the garden is never one and done. Even in the most successful growing seasons all participants need to review and assess whether any changes are necessary -- new conditions (like climate change!), emerging trends or markets (a new all-local restaurant coming that wants more of your tomatoes), to cite a few examples. It's never finished, there's always a new season with new challenges and if you don't want to revert to a totally overgrown and thorny, ugly mess, you have to keep improving.

IF NOT YOU, THEN WHO? IF NOT NOW, THEN WHEN?

— Hillel

THE TILLERS

Tillers are the visionaries, the pioneers. They are usually the first ones in. They can easily see what is not there, but can be. Because of their ability to see what will be, they are willing to do the pre-work, often alone, misunderstood and unappreciated. They are determined and seek to enable change that will last. Their goal is to create a foundation for growth. They survey the land, identify the best spot for the garden, and go to work with little fanfare, focused on the need to disrupt what exists in order to create the space for new growth.

Tillers work hard and long and rely on their own sense of purpose and self-motivation to reward their labor. They usually catch the attention of others and are sometimes ridiculed and misunderstood by those who are satisfied with the status quo or fail to see the vision that drives the tiller.

The tiller is future-focused and can't be too concerned with what is or was beyond their understanding of what needs to be done now. They can't be bothered by their detractors. They simply ignore them, and like a horse with blinders, they plod forward focused on the singular task ahead of breaking up the shallow surface of the soil to prepare it for the seed planters who will follow.

Once the soil is tilled and the foundation is ready for planting, tillers consider it done and prefer to move on to the next plot of unbroken ground. The breaking of the ground is cause enough for celebration for them.

Tillers are tactful, thick-skinned, and will work with almost anyone who is willing to get their hands dirty alongside them, including the planters who follow in their footsteps. But not the weed pullers. They fear the weed pullers. Tillers fear weed pullers because they know they may be misperceived as a weed because they are such patient tillers. Tillers also tend to find weedpullers to be too divisive.

THE PLANTERS

The planters see the freshly tilled ground as an invitation to sow seeds and plant. They are motivated and optimistic about the future. They excitedly share their vision and passion in verbal pictures of "what will be if we all work together." Others around them find their enthusiasm and positivity motivating and inspirational. The inclusive nature of planters allows them to easily recruit others to work alongside them. They are happy to meet people where they are and find a place for everyone. They know and understand the complexities and particulars of the garden, as well as the specific needs of plants, and work hard to create a space with room for all. They are optimistic and determined that all of their hard work will eventually result in a bountiful harvest. This is their big-picture motivation. While they recognize that weeds may pop up, they never let the weeds occupy too much of their attention. They are willing to tolerate some weeds as long as they don't distract greatly from the ultimate harvest. They would rather manage the weeds than eliminate them.

Planters are so busy celebrating every small step and eagerly anticipating the impending harvest that they often forget that their success wouldn't be possible if it weren't for the tillers who came before them and the weed pullers who work alongside them. They acknowledge the weed pullers are necessary, but silently wish they'd pull the weeds in a quieter, less-disruptive manner.

THE WEED PULLERS

The weed pullers are the realists of the garden. They save the celebration for the evidence of true progress and are happy to challenge any systems standing in the way of progress. They have a keen eye for spotting where the work needs to be done. They see all weeds as an

immediate threat that must be removed from the roots by nearly any means, even if some of the garden is damaged in the process. To them, the results justify the means. They are more concerned about the absence of weeds than the presence of the garden. They have perfectionistic tendencies. They are action and results-oriented. They operate with a "What's next?" or "What's missing?" mindset.

Weed pullers are not people pleasers. They are driven by a larger purpose - stomping out weeds at all cost. They will gladly push others out of the garden if they feel they are impeding progress. The threat of losing friends does not deter them. They are perfectly happy to work alone if necessary, rather than collaborate with others who don't share their passion for a completely weed-free garden. They praise other weed pullers but are quick to encourage cancel culture – just cancel or dismiss everyone if it is deemed necessary for the good of the garden. This causes others to view them as insensitive and tactless. Weed pullers are often heard saying "It's not my job to teach you."

Think about the descriptors of tillers, planters and weed pullers. Do you identify with one role? Do you play all of these positions based on the situation? Either way, identify

the best fit, take that role and run with it. Regardless of what role(s) you believe you play in the garden of inclusion, whatever you do, IGNORE. THE. PASSIVE. OBSERVER. There are people who will not till, they won't plant and they have no interest in pulling weeds. However, they will in their passive observation make comments for how other people should go about tilling, planting, and pulling weeds. Do not allow these people to distract you. Trust that they will engage once it's harvest time. For now, work around them. You will waste energy checking in and trying to appease them. So don't try. They are dead weight and will do nothing but drag down the effort.

THERE IS HOPE FOR OUR GARDEN

What role will you play? Are you a tiller, a planter or a weed puller? Which role best suits your talents and temperament? Because success – a bountiful harvest from the garden of diversity, equity, and inclusion – requires each individual's gifts and commitment. A microcosm, if you will, of the very culture you are seeking to create!

There is hope for our gardens, but only if we work together with clear purpose and sustained commitment. Just as a garden must be cultivated in order to survive, we must be purposeful about cultivating culture within our workplaces in order for us to reap the benefits of diversity, equity, and inclusion efforts. Farming has never been a spectator sport. It takes work from all of us who have a desire to bring the best of ourselves and our colleagues to bear, every single day.

And it's important that we do. If we want to eat, we need farmers who know how to bring all the right talents together to till the ground, plant the seeds, pull the weeds and reap the harvest. If we want our organizations to thrive today and into tomorrow, bringing the diverse experiences, talents and perspectives of all to the table.

As I said earlier, my strengths do not lie in the realm of the tiller. Perhaps my pepper plants would have thrived –

maybe we'd all be eating green peppers from my garden right now -- if I'd had the foresight to engage others to bring their skills to the effort.

I know better now. And so do you.

If not you, then who? If not now, when?

PART THREE: Assessments

TILLERS: PATH-CLEARERS

- Are you willing to be the only person representing your group in an organization, on a team, in a neighborhood, etc.?

- Do you have thick skin? Can you withstand other people's unfair criticism? Ignorant judgmental comments?

- Have you or are you open to marrying outside your race or class?

- Are you willing to clear or "till" a path that you may never be able to walk on or get credit for?

- Are you driven by a sense of self-determination and self- efficacy?

PLANTERS: SEEDS OF CHANGE

- Are you willing to work with a diverse group of people to reach a shared goal?

- Is the work you're doing building on the work of several others?

- You challenge the status quo by using a diverse group of allies?

- Do you tend to be sensitive or empathetic and that is the impetus for doing the work?

- Are you driven by a sense of diversity, belonging and inclusion?

WEED PULLERS:
REVOLUTIONARY DISRUPTORS

- Are you willing to fall on a sword for your people?

- Are you willing to destroy entire systems to reach the ultimate goal?

- Do you value healthy conflict and battles if it challenges issues of immorality?

- Does your vision tend to make other people uncomfortable and that is not your primary concern?

- Are you driven by a sense of fairness, social justice and equity?

REFERENCES

- "The harvest is plentiful" quote
  The Holy Bible in the Book of Matthew, Chapter 9, Verse 35

- Progress followed by regression
  Dr. Ibram Kendi in "Stamped From the Beginning"

- Lifting up rocks to see dirty worms
  Jim Collins in "Good to Great"

- "If not you, then who? If not now, when?" quote
  Hillel, first-century Jewish scholar

ABOUT THE AUTHORS

DR. NICOLE D. PRICE helps difference get along. She is the creator of a successful diversity and inclusion workshop, which has been conducted with hundreds of people from various backgrounds all across the United States. Her strategy uses private, reflective practice (like this book) to do the "hard" work, which then allows for a much more productive and fruitful, way-forward discussion within group settings. Learn more about her company and work at: www.livelyparadox.com.

JOEL BARRETT is an LGBTQ speaker and writer. He is recognized for his colorful storytelling as a former Baptist pastor and survivor of ex-gay therapy. Joel has a unique ability to bring people together, but it was his voice and experience with farming and gardening that helped to create this project.

Made in the USA
Monee, IL
30 October 2020